THE TASTE OF FROZEN TEARS

The Taste of Frozen Tears:
My Antarctic Walkabout-
A Graphic Novel

Jessica Johns
Tyler Hein
Ed. E. Snyder
Austin Mardon
Catherine Mardon

Clare Dalton

First Printing: 2020

Typeset and Cover Design by Clare Dalton

Book cover font: *The Fell Types are digitally reproduced by Igino Marini. www.iginomarini.com*

ISBN 978-1-77369-203-6

Golden Meteorite Press

103 11919 82 St NW

Edmonton, AB T5B 2W3

www.goldenmeteoritepress.com

Contents

The book you are about to read is published by Golden Meteorite Press, a subsidiary of the Antarctic Institute of Canada. The AIC is a non-profit Canadian charity organization founded and operated by partners Austin and Catherine Mardon.
It has been adapted into a graphic novel by Clare Dalton.

*"No temptation has overtaken you except what is common to mankind.
And God is faithful; he will not let you be tempted beyond what you can bear.
But when you are tempted, he will also provide a way out so that you can endure it."*
— 1 Corinthians 10:13.

*"If your head explodes with dark forebodings too;
I'll see you on the dark side of the moon."*
- Pink Floyd: "Brain Damage"

CHAPTER 1

The ANSMET Program

University of Lethbridge, September. 1981.

Austin Mardon was a Geology major in the bachelor of science program. He took several courses in Polar Geography and Polar Sciences.

In 1985 he took a Remote Sensing course.

Digital remote sensing and image analysis. Environmental applications of using satellite data for earth observation gained from aerial photography. The scanning of the earth by aircraft or satellite (including drones or side-saddled cameras attached to helicopters or planes) in order to obtain information about the surveyed territory.

Austin was supposed to write a paper for this class, but he was flipping through Discover magazine instead.

Ursula Marvin was an American planetary geologist and the author of Continental Drift: Evolution of a Concept published in 1973.
She worked at the Smithsonian Astrophysical Observatory and was a key contributor in her studies of meteorites and lunar samples.

There was an article was about research related to her 1984 expedition to Antarctica on an ANSMET survey,

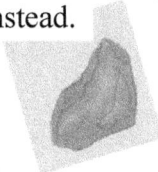

where she analyzed the first lunar meteorite from Allan Hills.

The ANSMET (Antarctic Search for Meteorites) program, led by William Cassidy, was dedicated to the collection of meteorites from Antarctica. In the article, Ursula describes riding snowmobiles to retrieve meteorites.

Snowmobiles? Seems tedious.

WHAT IF:
REMOTE SENSING
+
AERIAL PHOTO. TO
SURVEY LARGE AREAS
- BIRD'S EYE VIEW TO
FIND METEORITES
- LESSEN TIME SPENT
ON THE GROUND

Dear Dr. Marvin,

My name is Austin Mardon and I have a question and an idea about the collection of meteorites by the

He thought of an idea, then he wrote a letter.

Ursula was ecstatic with this proposal and suggested he contact Dr. William Cassidy-so he did.

Cassidy responded, asking for more detail.

Austin argued that this new method of meteorite recovery would be more cost-effective, save time, and would minimize time on the ground in harsh, dangerous environments.

Bill Cassidy created the ANSMET program when he discovered that Antarctica was a meteorite goldmine.

Meteorites are a major reason we know what we know about the formation and early history of the solar system.

March came and went without a second response from Cassidy.

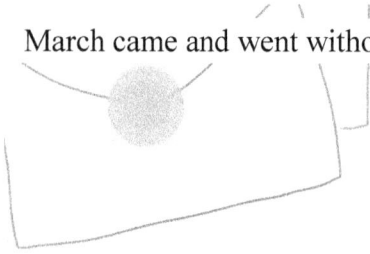

In June, Austin graduated his bachelor's degree.

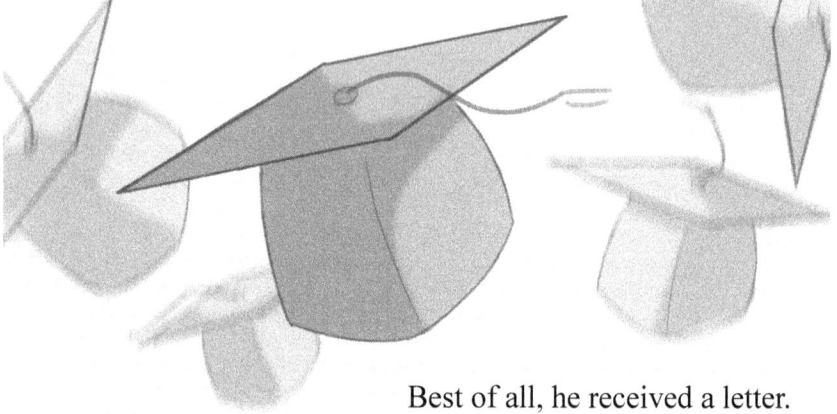

Best of all, he received a letter.

Austin,
That's a great proposal.
I would love to have you along on an
ANSMET survey after you have finished your
graduate degree.

I recommend that you apply for a graduate
program in Geography in order to be better
prepared for research in the Antarctic.
Please let me know what you think, and I
look forward to hearing back from you. I will
be in contact if you decide to go forward
with my offer.

Regards,
William Cassidy

Luckily, Austin had already applied and been accepted to the University of South Dakota.

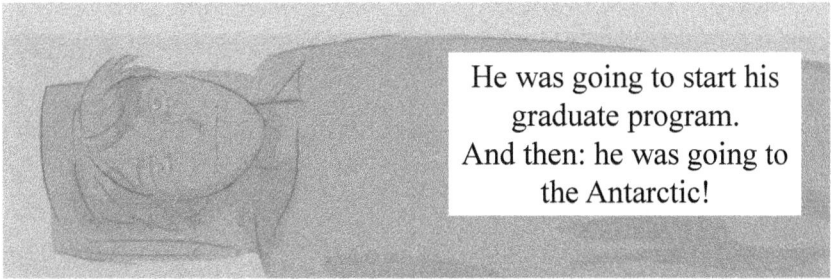

He was going to start his graduate program.
And then: he was going to the Antarctic!

Lethbridge, Alberta

Vermilion, South Dakota

Hey! Austin right? I'm Raj. What program are you in?
Geography. You?
Poetry.
So... what do you want to do with geography?
Actually, I'm going to the Antarctic in a year.
YOU'RE GOING WHERE?!
I'm going on a survey to test out a theory I have about locating meteorites.
Meteorites?! Wow...I'm studying Rumi.
My *roomie* is studying *Rumi?*
Oh, very funny.

Austin's graduate school life began-stressful as he had anticipated.

Are you excited to go home?

Not really. Christmas isn't always a great time.

Oh, not happy about seeing family?

I am! I miss them. It's just that Christmases for me aren't always the perfect family events that you see in movies, you know?

AUSTIN!

Hey, dad.

Christmas Eve.

The priest gave a sermon on the plight of the Magi.

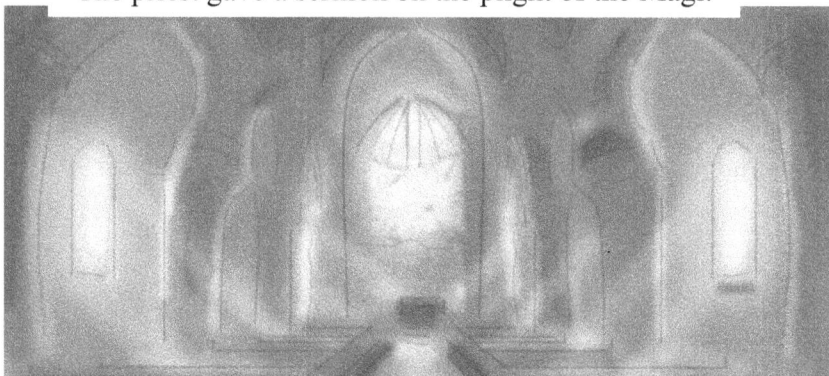

Following a star they knew would lead to something special.

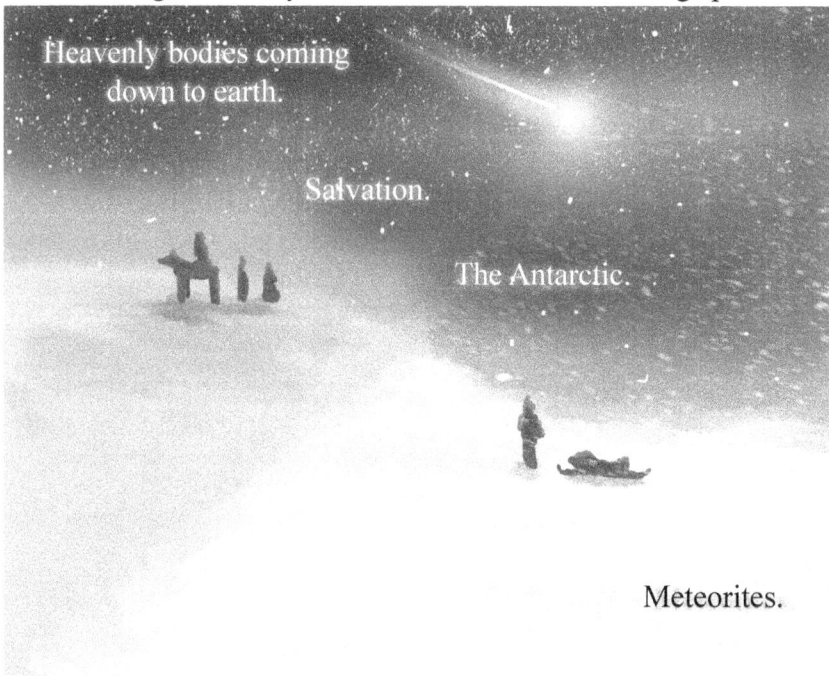

Heavenly bodies coming down to earth.

Salvation.

The Antarctic.

Meteorites.

Dad....I'm going to apply for my PhD at the University of Texas Agriculture and Mining.

I'll support whatever you choose to do, but are you sure about this?

I am.

...Texas is nice.

I think you'll have a lot to offer.

CHAPTER 2

Acceptance

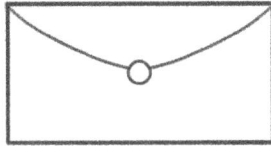

A. Madden

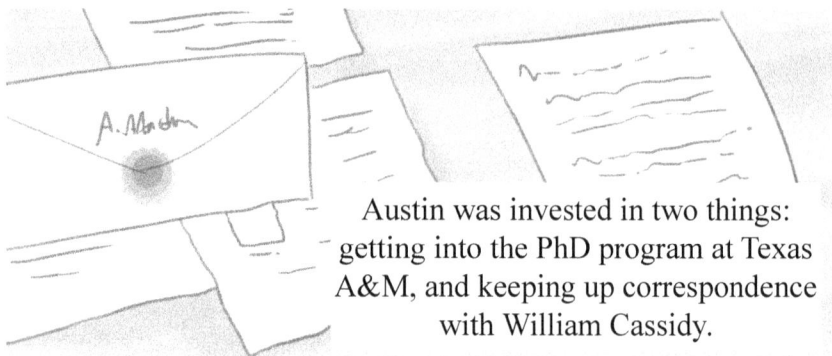

Austin was invested in two things: getting into the PhD program at Texas A&M, and keeping up correspondence with William Cassidy.

His admission letter came in April.

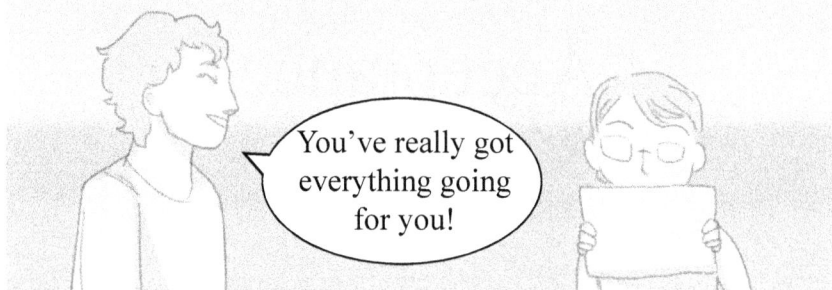

You've really got everything going for you!

The second letter from William Cassidy came in May.

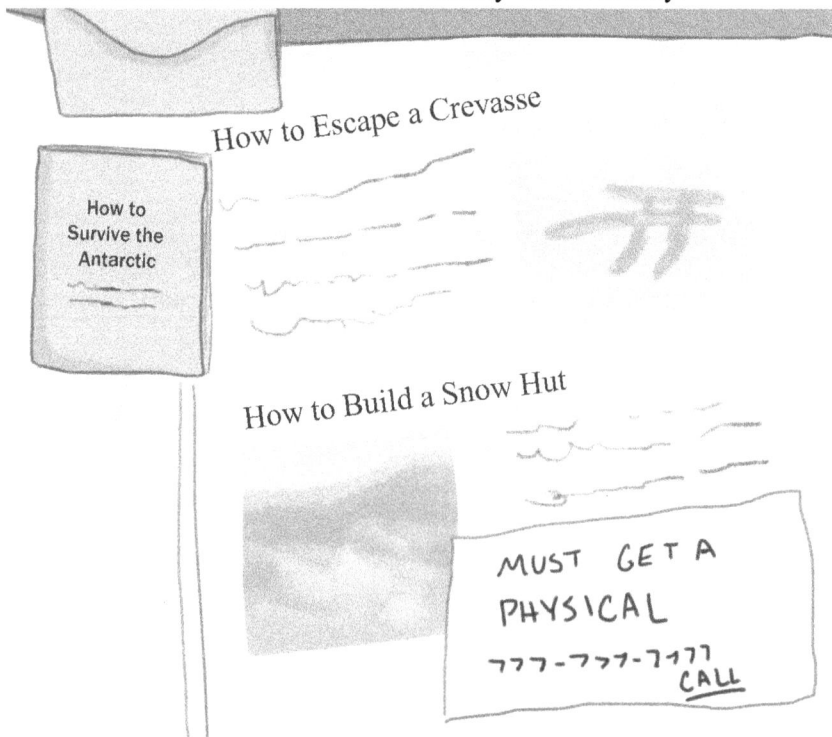

How to Escape a Crevasse

How to Survive the Antarctic

How to Build a Snow Hut

MUST GET A PHYSICAL
777-777-7777
CALL

Nowitzki.
Uh, hello Dr. Nowitzki. My name is Austin Mardon-
Oh yes, Bill told me you'd be calling. Accompanying Dr. Cassidy to the Antarctic right away?
1 2 3 4 5 8 9

Uh, yes sir. Due to leave in November.
Great, great. I just have a couple questions here for your file with them. Does extreme weather affect you?
Uh, no? Sorry Doctor, can I ask what is this for?
Oh! This is a psychological evaluation, to make sure you're mentally fit for travel.

Oh.

Does anyone in your family have a
history of mental illness?

No.

This was not true.

Have you ever had a psychotic episode or
been admitted into a mental health facility?

No.

This was true.

Have you ever thought about
committing the act of suicide?

No.

Was this true?

Well that's it.

That's it?

You seem fit to go. I'll send this
off to Bill. Take care now!

After the psychological evaluation was the physical.

Hello, Austin. We're going to do a full physical on you today. It will be a bit **strenuous.**

I see in your records that this information is going to the NSF, so we'll get that off as soon as possible. Open your mouth please.

We're going to look at your vitals first: blood pressure, heart rate, and respiratory. I'll take your temperature.

We'll also run urinalysis, take a blood count, and give your lipids a lookie-lou. And of course we'll check your nethers. We'll be testing you for HIV AIDS; if you are positive, you'll be immediately disqualified from the ANSMET program. But a good Alberta boy like you? I'm not worried. You'll be interested to know that you're one of the first people in Alberta to be tested for it. Won't that make your parents proud? Haw haw! I'm only kidding. The last things I'll have you do are turn your head and cough to test for a hernia, and then we'll examine your prostate. Lots to do. It's all a bit strenuous, but at least then you'll know.

27

Strenuous didn't even begin to describe it.

CHAPTER 3
Bill Cassidy

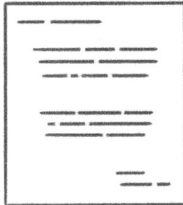

Summer.

Keep in touch, okay Austin?

I will, Raj.

Austin began to prepare mentally and physically for the journey.

College Station, Texas. August.

September. He met his professors at a mixer held off campus.

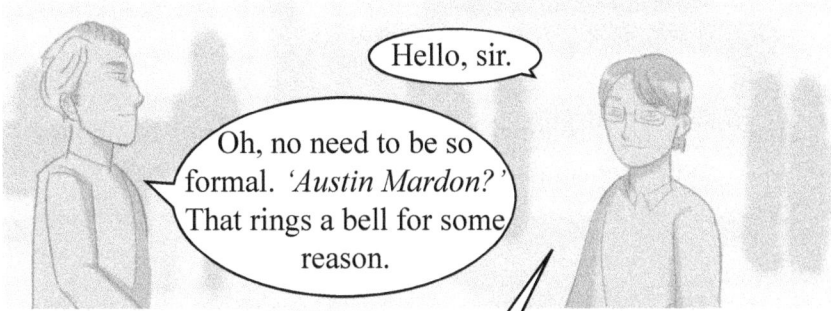

Hello, sir.

Oh, no need to be so formal. *'Austin Mardon?'* That rings a bell for some reason.

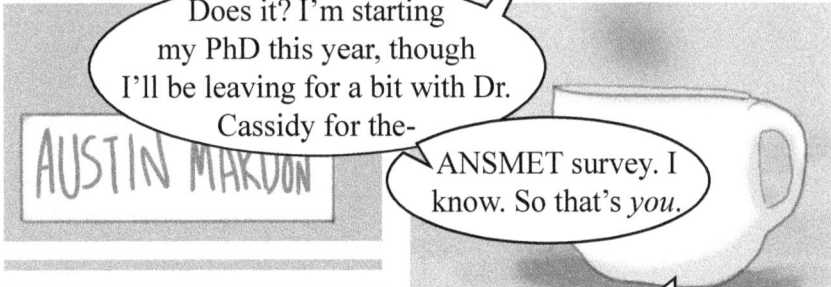

Does it? I'm starting my PhD this year, though I'll be leaving for a bit with Dr. Cassidy for the-

AUSTIN MARDON

ANSMET survey. I know. So that's *you.*

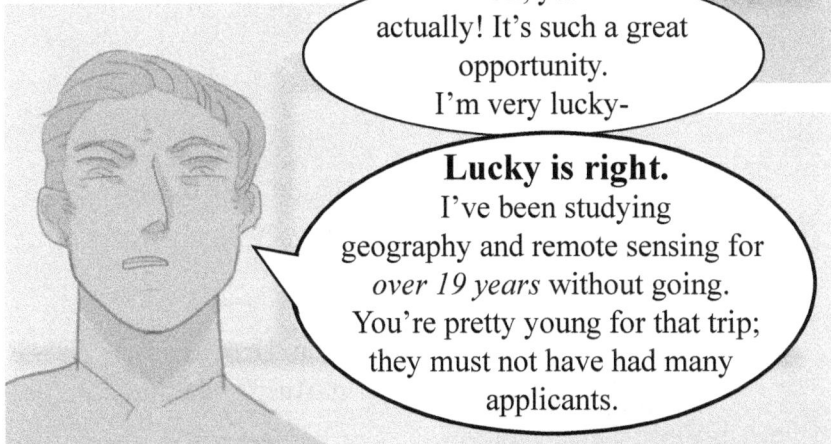

Oh, yes actually! It's such a great opportunity. I'm very lucky-

Lucky is right. I've been studying geography and remote sensing for *over 19 years* without going. You're pretty young for that trip; they must not have had many applicants.

...Uh, it was nice meeting you.

I have to go.

His professor's comments really rattled his confidence.

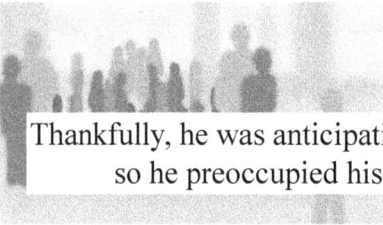

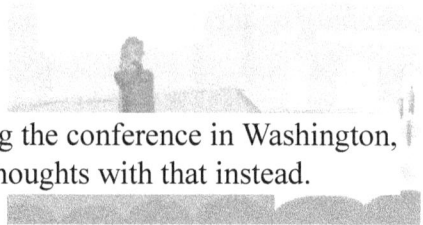

Thankfully, he was anticipating the conference in Washington, so he preoccupied his thoughts with that instead.

Austin recognized William Cassidy even before the moderator introduced him.

Hello, Dr. Cassidy. I'm Austin Mardon.

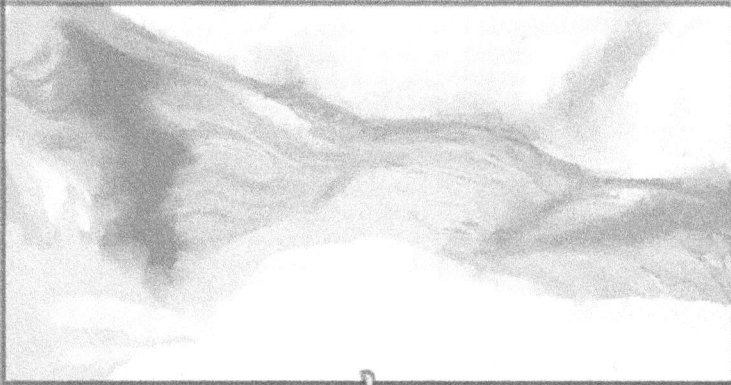

CHAPTER 4

Preparation

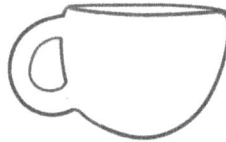

Late September. There was too much toxicity and petty jealousy among the people in his department, so he switched to the Educational Geography program.

Everyone was emotionally supportive, and welcomed him quickly.

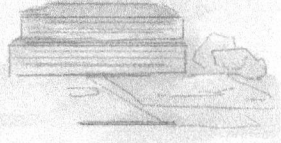

Austin! We were going to do the whole surprise thing. You're early!

I'm only gone a couple months! You didn't have to...

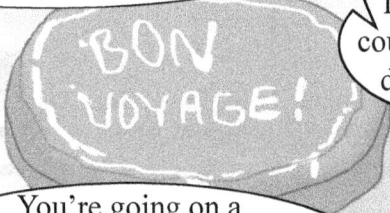

BON VOYAGE!

You're going on a trip of a lifetime! The least we could do is have a little cake before you leave.

We got you a little something for your snowmobile!

Houston to Honolulu

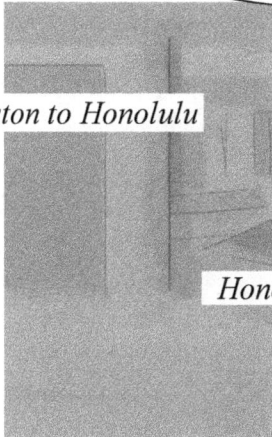

Honolulu to Auckland

Auckland. With two hours before his flight to Christchurch, he was meeting with his uncle Francis.

AUSTIN!
I know you have to get back to school once this is over, but if you want a holiday before you go home, I'd love for you to stay with me.
I don't know what to say.
You don't have to answer now. Think on it. Write. Take care.
Auckland to Christchurch
He was due to meet up with everyone tomorrow.

Keizo Yanai.

Christian Koeberl.

Luke Lindner.

John Scott.

He woke up early for morning walks and stopped for a sausage roll on his two days in Christchurch.

It's time.

Once, a group of researchers who'd had too much fun the night before fell asleep on the flight. They didn't realize the plane had turned around due to weather. They woke up and walked out in winter gear to 30 degrees in Christchurch.

That's hilarious—

It isn't.
Those men weren't taking the expedition seriously from the start. It was foolish. This isn't just some fun adventure. **This is serious, dangerous work.**

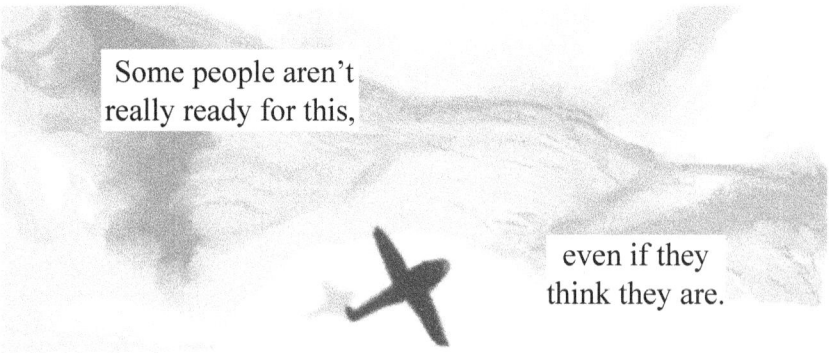

Some people aren't really ready for this,

even if they think they are.

CHAPTER 5

Antarctica

McMurdo Station is the largest community in Antarctica.

It was to be the new home base for Austin and the crew of the 1986 ANSMET Antarctic Meteorite Recovery Expedition.

On the icy runway were two coffins. It was a grim reminder of Bill Cassidy's warning.

As if to further reinforce his words about the serious nature of the expedition- Cassidy received word that his mother had died while they were traveling.

He phoned his wife to make burial arrangements.

Then he went into his room with instructions not to be disturbed,

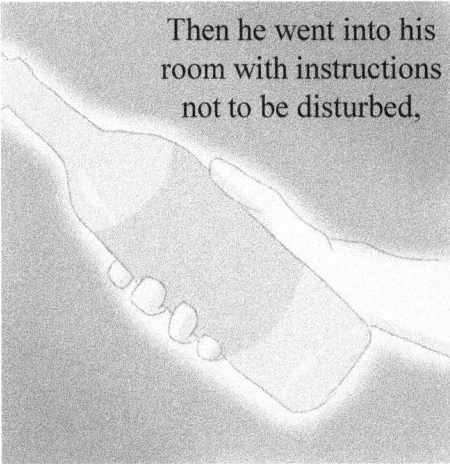

to grieve the sudden loss of his mother, half the world away.

So, on the first day Austin, unaware of the current status of the expedition, found himself with time to explore his new, unfamiliar surroundings.

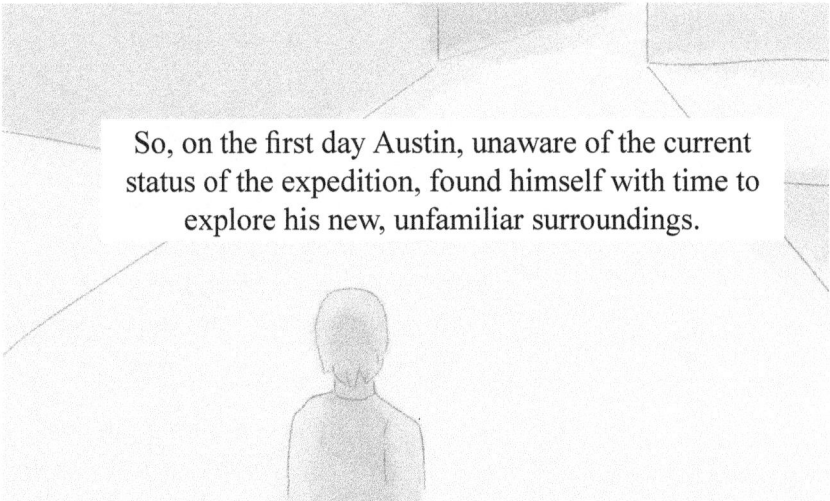

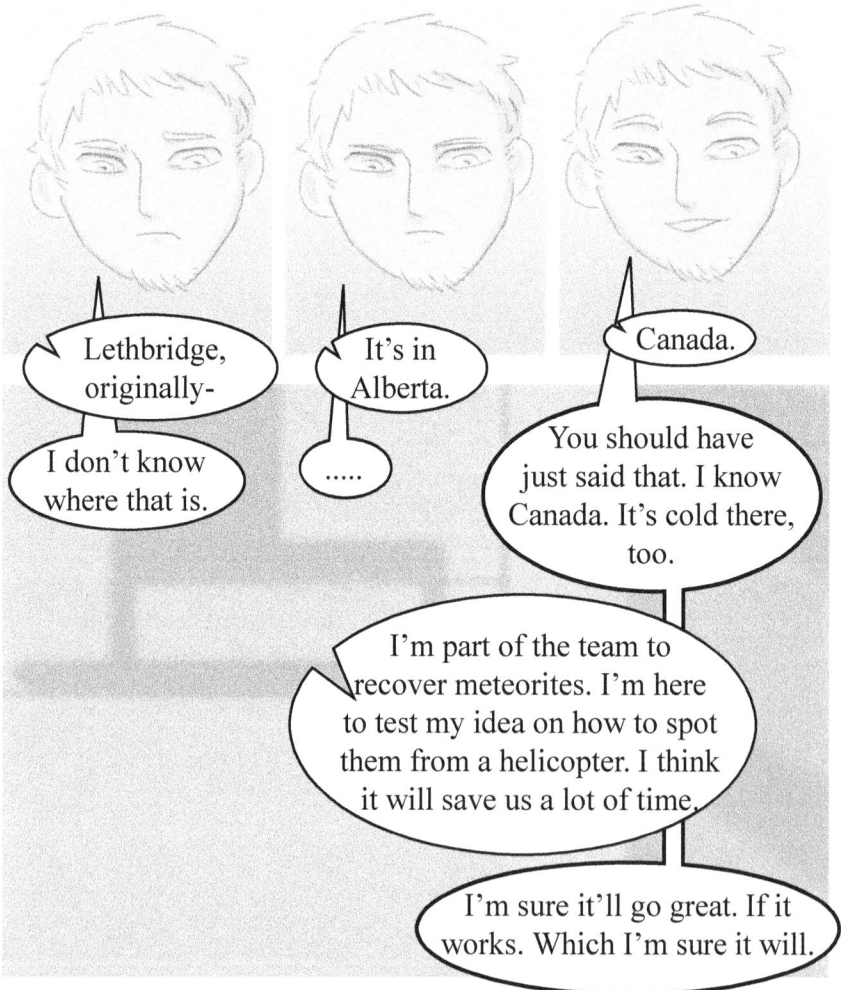

CHAPTER 6

Free Ride

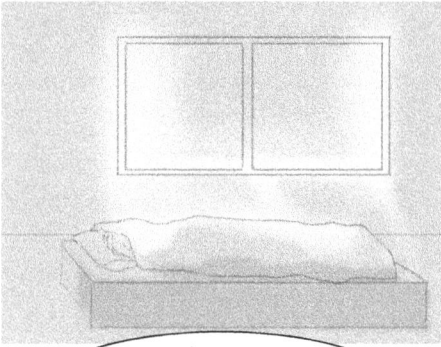

Good morning.
Are we flying to Lewis
Cliff tonight?

No. No one's seen
Bill since he heard
about his mom.

Do you think
he's okay?

Would you be?

I'm honestly a bit
surprised he only
took one bottle.

With his second day
free, Austin decided to
trek to Scott Base,
the New Zealand
research station.

When he finally arrived, he was greeted warmly by the New Zealand researchers and spent a good part of his day touring around.

Austin began trudging back to McMurdo from Scott Base.

Are you on your way to McMurdo?

Slowly, but surely!

Want a lift? I'm almost done here. Name's Clark.

Don't focus on the ground.

Why not?

No good markers of distance. You lose track of time. Like highway hypnosis, but worse. You get lost in it.

It was the same sensation of becoming unstuck from the present that Austin would feel on long Alberta drives.

Fields of wheat and canola, the stillness of the horizon broken only by run-down grain elevators.

They blend together and trap the senses. Highway hypnosis. Even in Antarctica.

Do you want to fly the helicopter?

What? No. I would rather not.

It's simple. You'll be fine. Here. All you have to do is steer. Just focus on keeping it steady.

I hear you got caught horsing around.
Ah. Yes. I'm sorry about that.
I told them I'd speak with you so he would stop talking. Not sure why they made such a big deal about it.
You're not mad?
No. There's far worse things you could be doing.
I guess so. I'm sorry if it caused you any hassle.
No hassle. Get some sleep. We're going to begin tomorrow, so be ready in the morning.
MCMURDO STATION ANTARCTICA
MCMURDO STATION
NOV 1986
AIR POST NOV 1986

CHAPTER 7

Safety Checks

I didn't realize you could can bread.

You'd be surprised. It's possible to can almost anything. They get creative.

Are we taking this to Scott's Hut tomorrow?

No. This is for later field research but we're packing it now. Tomorrow is a chance for you to see some history.

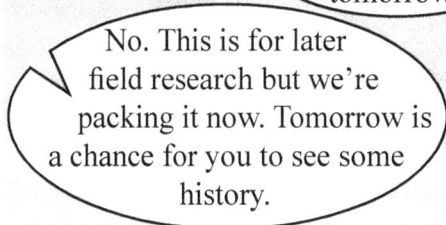

What do you say? We'll all head out to one of the big peaks and summit it. Let's call it team bonding. Keizo?

I'm not climbing a mountain, John. We can just agree now to be friends.

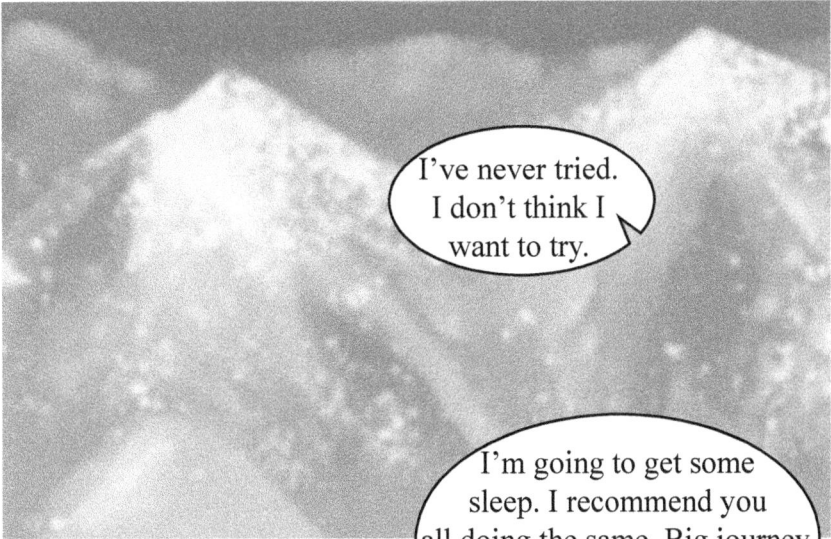

CHAPTER 8

Scott's Hut

5:18

Good morning, Bill. What's the plan for today?

History lesson.

We're going learn how to quickly make camp, and sleep out in the tents tonight, by Scott's Hut. Learn how to run the sleds. Learn how to unpack, pack, and unpack again. Bunch of learning. It'll be exciting.

Scott's Hut, Ross Island:
Built for Terra Nova Expedition,
World Historic Site.

Robert Falcon Scott and a small crew set out in a race against Roald Admundsen's expedition to be the first men to reach the South Pole.

But they were too late.

Depleted of resources, energy, and spirit, they all perished on the return journey. The journals recovered from their frozen bodies detailed Scott as an obsessive, reckless leader who took liberties with the lives of the crew to achieve his goal.

CHAPTER 9

Secret Success

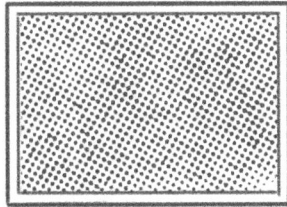

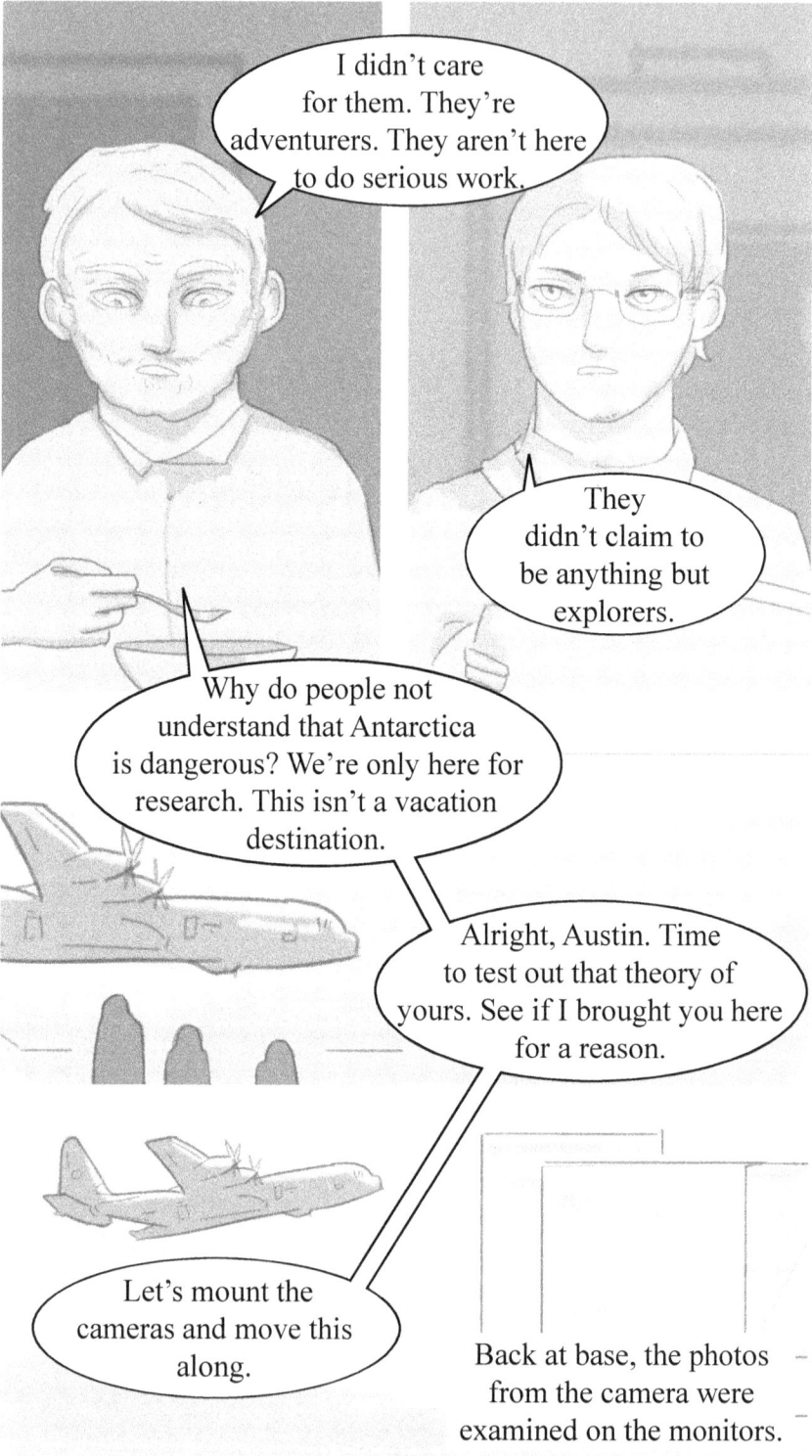

I didn't care for them. They're adventurers. They aren't here to do serious work.

They didn't claim to be anything but explorers.

Why do people not understand that Antarctica is dangerous? We're only here for research. This isn't a vacation destination.

Alright, Austin. Time to test out that theory of yours. See if I brought you here for a reason.

Let's mount the cameras and move this along.

Back at base, the photos from the camera were examined on the monitors.

Well, the technology works. That's good. But we can't get the quality high enough to make heads or tails of anything in these photographs.
Sorry everyone.
It's alright, mate. That's science for you.
A cruel mistress.
How are you feeling?
Good. Well, I mean… I'm okay.
Mind if I sit? You shouldn't be disappointed.
Why not? My experiment failed. It's the whole reason you brought me on this expedition.

Yes, but that's how it goes sometimes. Plus, the technology worked. You should take solace in that. Perhaps you're simply ahead of your time.

Thanks.

I mean it. You shouldn't let this get you down. Think of it as a secret success.

Secret success?

It'll be viable eventually. It just wasn't in the cards for this expedition. Besides, we can recover meteorites the old-fashioned way. Nothing wrong with that.

I mean it. I'm pleased with how things went. There's no shame in attempting something new. It's how research moves forward. You did good. We're finding meteorites tomorrow. It's going to be exciting.

CHAPTER 10

First Meteorites

Beardmore Glacier is one of the largest valley glaciers in the world.

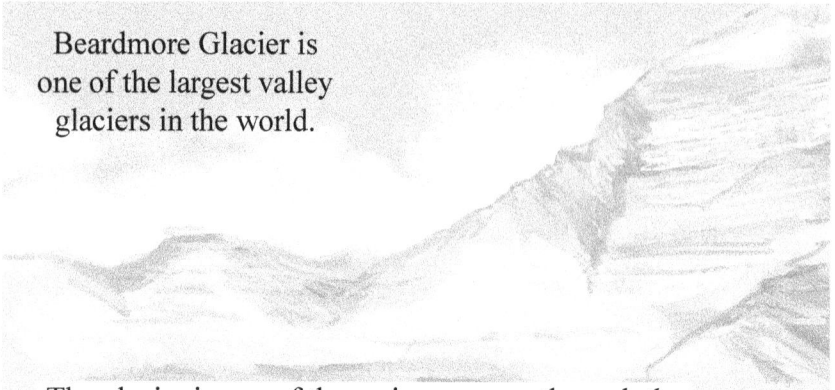

The glacier is one of the main passages through the Transantarctic mountain range to the great polar plateau beyond.

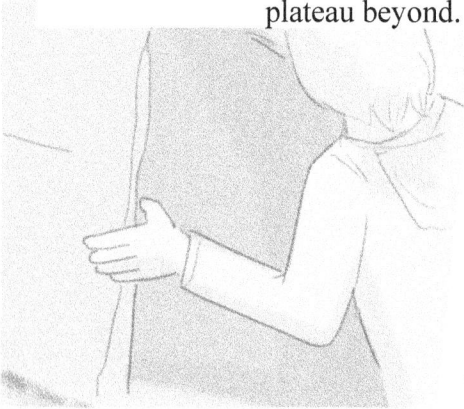

Austin and Keizo Yanai were partnered together in tents.

The Lewis Cliff Ice Tongue is located in the center of the Transantarctic Mountains.

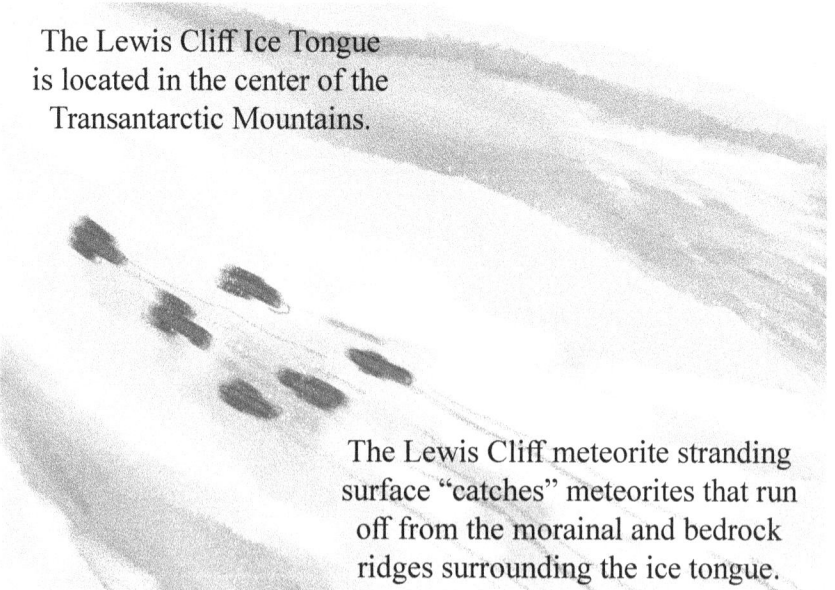

The Lewis Cliff meteorite stranding surface "catches" meteorites that run off from the morainal and bedrock ridges surrounding the ice tongue.

Welcome, everyone.

I apologize for all the delays. This is why
we all came here across the world. Get used
to the terrain, get accustomed to the area;
its waypoints, markers, signs, and signals.
Every day we're going to travel from base
camp to this area, where we're going to
drive around until we find a meteorite.
Then we're going to mark it with a stake,
bag it, tag it, and record it. Write everything
down, people. Then we survey the spots
where meteorites were found.
See if there are any patterns or similarities,
so maybe next time somebody can finally
figure out an easier way to do this.

Austin was beginning to
feel welcomed in
Antarctica.

Lost in thought, he sped up to an incline.

Climbing up the icy slope and calling out for John, Austin came to a realization.

Antarctica was not his friend.

CHAPTER 11

Fatigue

After the first week, where each day was full of first times, Austin's life fell into a daily routine.

Wake up.

Eat.

Scour the snow and ice for meteorites

Eat.

Scour again.

Return home.

Sleep. Repeat

Kind of underwhelming, aren't they? This is basically a field of rocks.

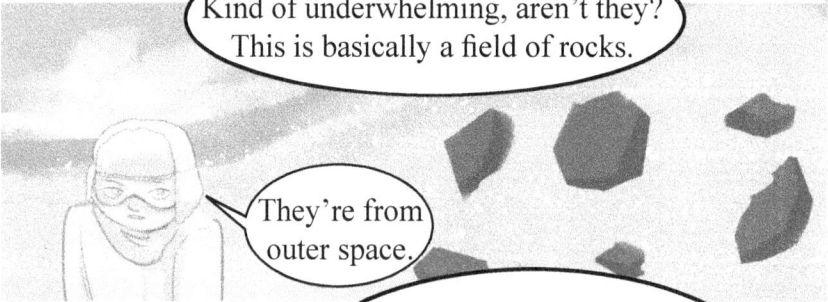

They're from outer space.

Pebbles from space are still only pebbles. Why aren't we on the moon? Why aren't we doing research up there?

I don't know what to tell you. This is the job.

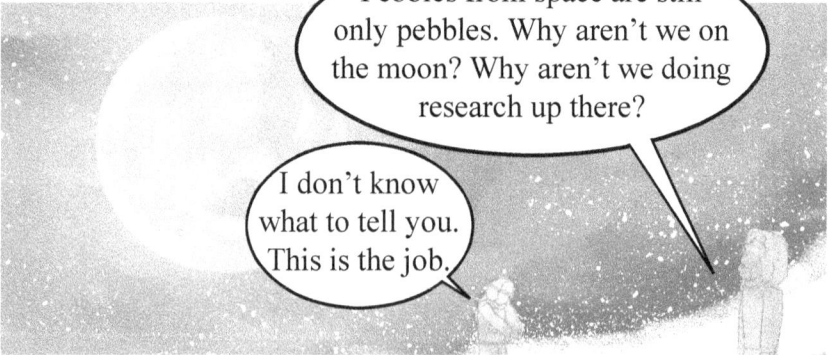

AUSTIN! STOP!

Austin...You've urinated on a lunar meteorite.

Huh?

One small drip for man...

Oh, come on.

Haha!

Three weeks into the expedition, Bill Cassidy searched an inner pocket in his parka and found a tuna fish sandwich— from their first flight to McMurdo.

A day later, the crew was on their way back to McMurdo from the field camp so that Bill Cassidy could get treatment for food poisoning.

Austin decided he should pay a visit to the medical area in McMurdo.

Hello Austin, my name is Dr. Jay. What brings you in to see me today?

My legs feel stiff all the time. The skin is hard; I don't have much feeling in them.

Okay, let's get a look at them. How long have you been here?

About a month.

Uh huh. What brings you to McMurdo?

Meteorite recovery.

With Dr. Cassidy, I'd bet. Find any?

Yeah, hundreds.

Just relax your muscles. Hundreds of meteorites? That's fantastic. Any dizziness? Nausea? Vomiting?

No. No vomiting or nausea. But I get dizzy spells. I haven't been sleeping well. The sun never goes down.

It definitely takes some getting used to. Do you tire quickly?
The work is tiring, but I don't think I tire easily. I'm losing weight.
That makes sense. You're working hard in heavy clothes. That probably isn't anything to worry about. You should think about is the bloodflow to your legs. Try doing some stretches in the morning and before bed.
Does this happen to everyone?
Everyone. Antarctica is tough on the body. You're going to be uncomfortable during your time here.

CHAPTER 12

Walking on Air

On one hand, he wanted to feel better about his current state due to Dr. Jay's assertion that his experience was normal.

But on the other hand, how could it be considered normal? Is it normal to feel your capabilities slip away from you?

He thought about Robert Falcon Scott and his crew of doomed men. At least Austin had something tangible. He could see a meteorite, balance its weight in his palm, feel the rough edges with his fingers.

Scott and his men marched to their death to...plant a flag? It was clear how destroyed they were by not arriving first, even though it wouldn't have saved them.

At least they would have had something, a small token to hold with them while Antarctica ground them down.

The men stood staring at him from the past and their pain felt present.

They eventually returned to their camp and resumed the mission.

Everything alright, John? You're lagging behind.

Yeah, I guess I didn't bind everything tightly enough. I'll catch up.

Alright. Austin, you wait with him. Go as a pair.

The damn things keep wobbling! You go ahead, Austin, I'll keep up.

John! There's a crevasse, watch out!
Go right! Go right! Go around!
I almost didn't see that hole.....
RUMBLE

A snow bridge. Suspended by trapped air, delaying it's collapse into the empty air below.

He looked down the steep drop where he had been standing moments earlier and saw his footprints still pressed in the snow far below.

Austin was lucky enough to have stepped off the bridge before it had fallen.

Austin. Jesus, man. Are you okay? It looked like you were levitating!

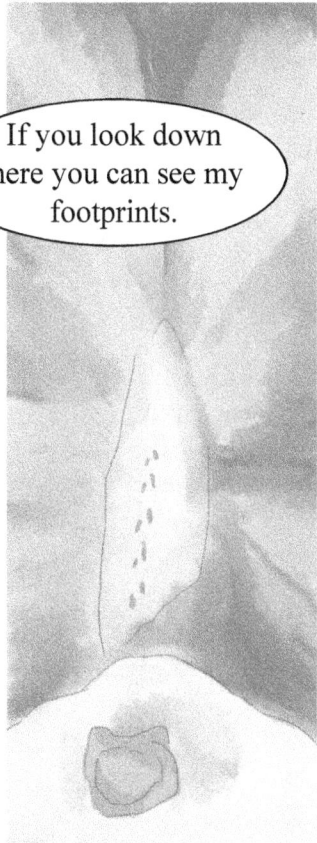

When he told the crew they would be venturing further south, through the Transantarctic Mountains, closer to the South Pole, Bill Cassidy said:

"Beyond the frozen seas are the frozen seas beyond the South Pole."

It was a strange way to alert the expedition team that the conditions they were enduring were about to get a whole lot worse.

Austin's physical condition worsened. His legs felt unconnected from his body.

Sometimes while the team was out in the field, Austin found himself crying.

One night, Austin tried counting sheep.

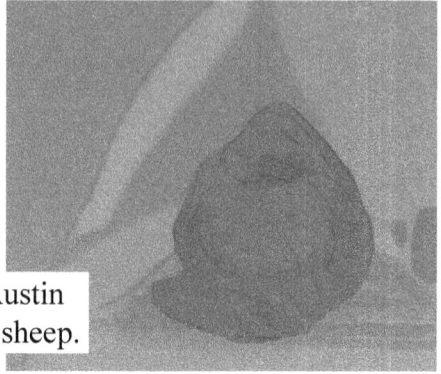

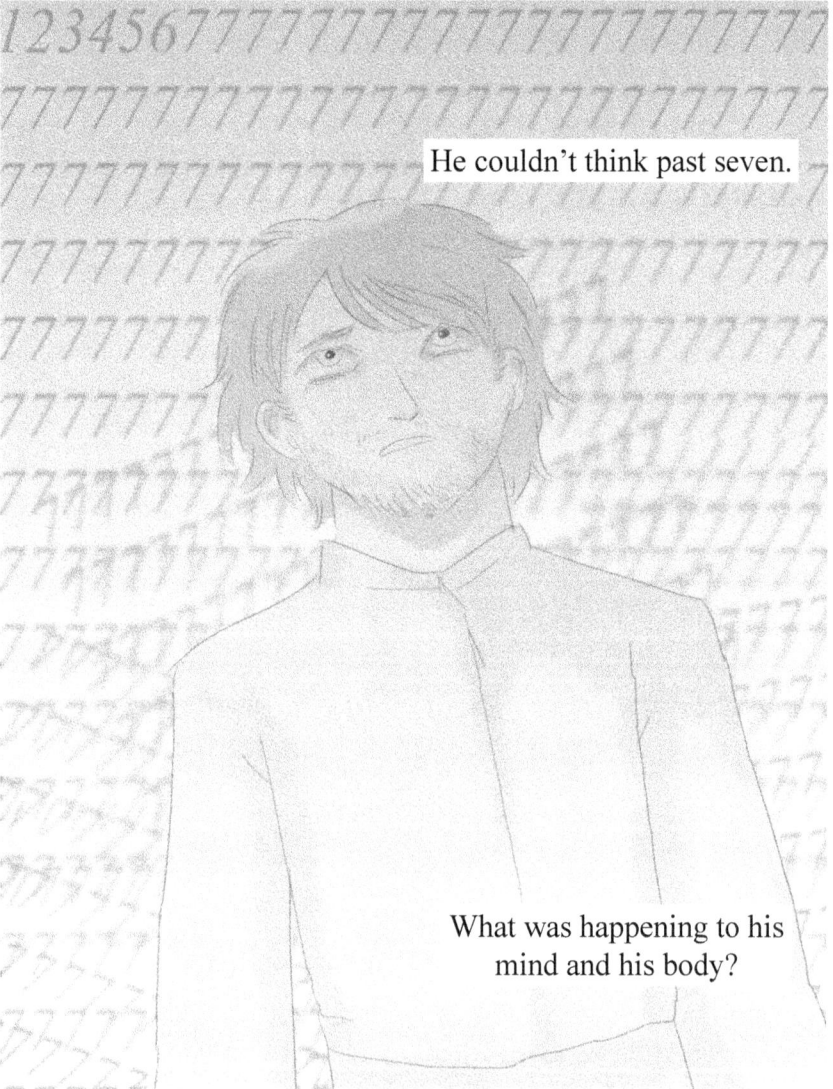

He couldn't think past seven.

What was happening to his mind and his body?

CHAPTER 13

Presents

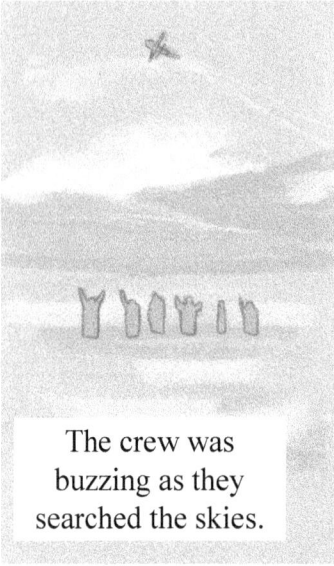

The crew was buzzing as they searched the skies.

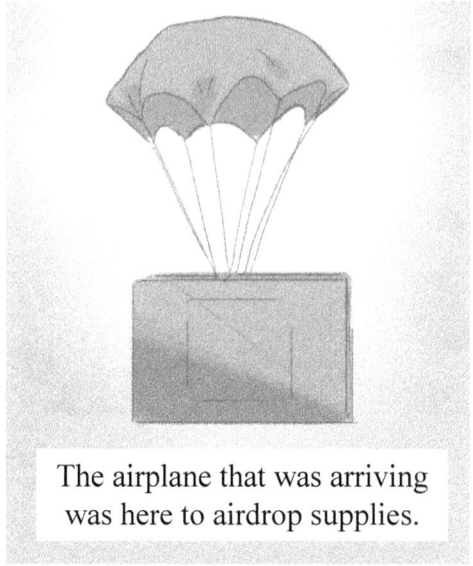

The airplane that was arriving was here to airdrop supplies.

The crate was brimming with reserves of food, fuel, and other necessary supplies.

A box of oranges? Man, I can't believe how much I missed fruit.

There was a letter from a friend of
his in South Dakota.

Hi Austin,
I guess you're in Antarctica? You should have
said something! You can't disappear with
out a goodbye and think we'd guess
Antarctica! Exciting! I hope all is going well
and this letter finds you in good spirits.
Hello from all your friends (and my
parents).

−Laurie

Austin held the letter
tenderly, touched by its
pleasant normalcy. Laurie
thought about him and
wished him well, and she
didn't seem worried.

It was the perfect
Christmas gift.

We're going to have a short day today. I have a surprise for dinner.

Merry Christmas! I know it's not much.

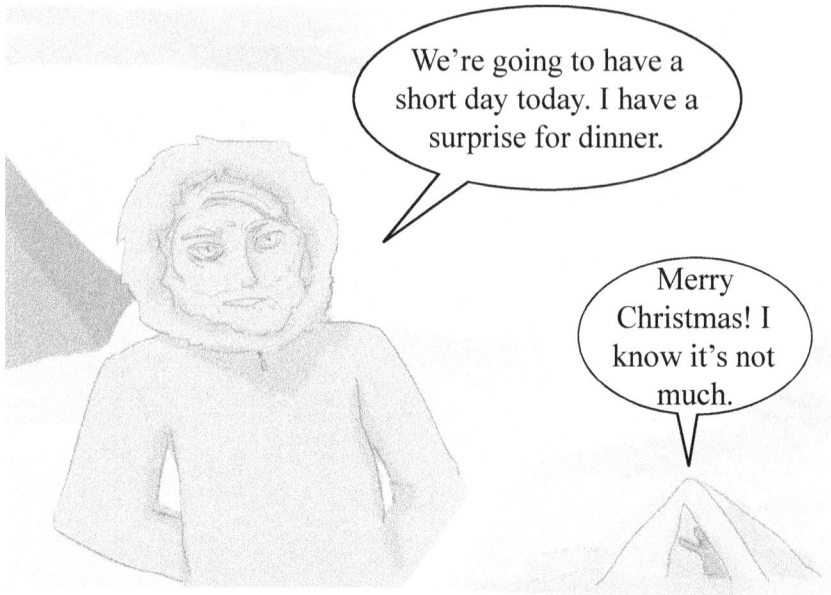

It was a such a mismatch of things, and it was doubtful that there was enough food to comfortably feed everyone, but Austin was grinning from ear to ear.

Everyone laughed and shared stories.

Each man spoke about his family and their traditions.

Bill Cassidy told them about the ancient history of Antarctica.

Luke shared his experiences living through the Second World War in Europe as a child.

Austin talked about his father and his father's father: they were professors. He felt it was *"written in the stars"* for him to continue the tradition.

He would learn and share what he'd learned, just as his father and grandfather had done.

"In the stars?"

"In the stars~"

Austin blushed, but he
laughed along with the men.
He knew it sounded silly.

He wasn't ready
for this experience
to end, but he was
looking forward to
getting back home.

He needed
direction; he
needed the stars.

New Years Eve rolled around. They
all had to be up early the next day.

It was the nearing the end of the season, as Austin stared into the largest meteorite he had ever seen.

Can someone come look at this? Bill? Bill, come over here.

Well I'll be. Luke! Bring an ice pick over here! And chisels and hammers, will ya? Great job.

I didn't really do anything.

You did enough. You did all that was asked of you. I told you to find a meteorite, and you found me a meteorite.

Austin went to his tent in high spirits, but as soon as he lied down he felt dizzy and delirious.

This had been worsening lately.
Headaches. His legs were
constantly cold to the touch.

He had given up
attempting to count past 7.

Even relieving his
bladder was painful.

When he looked at the
snow, he saw it was
stained blood red.

CHAPTER 14

Early Exit

The season was coming to an end, and Austin was a husk.

Austin, hello. Is there anything you need?

Ah, Bill. I'm worried. I keep… there's blood in my urine. I'm waking up with blood on my pillows. I think it's coming from out of my ears.

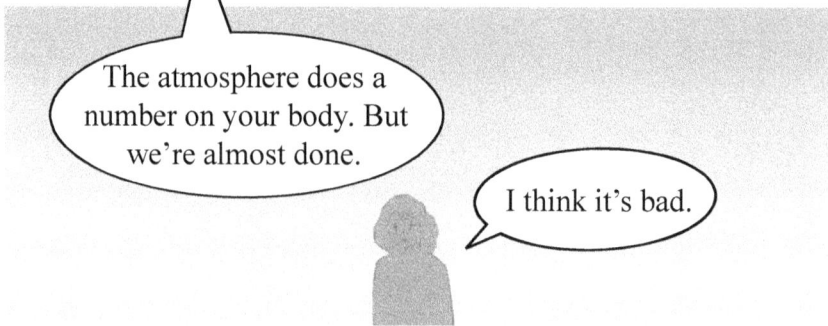

The atmosphere does a number on your body. But we're almost done.

I think it's bad.

Austin. I lost a toenail last night. Snapped right off in the cold. We make sacrifices for the kind of work that we do. The research requires it. It's cold. That's the way it is here.

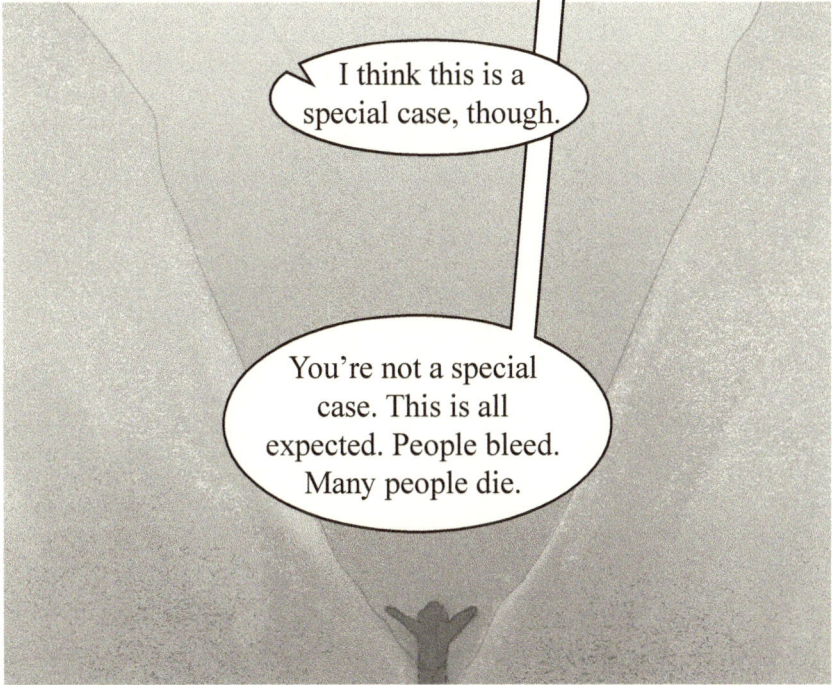

I think this is a special case, though.

You're not a special case. This is all expected. People bleed. Many people die.

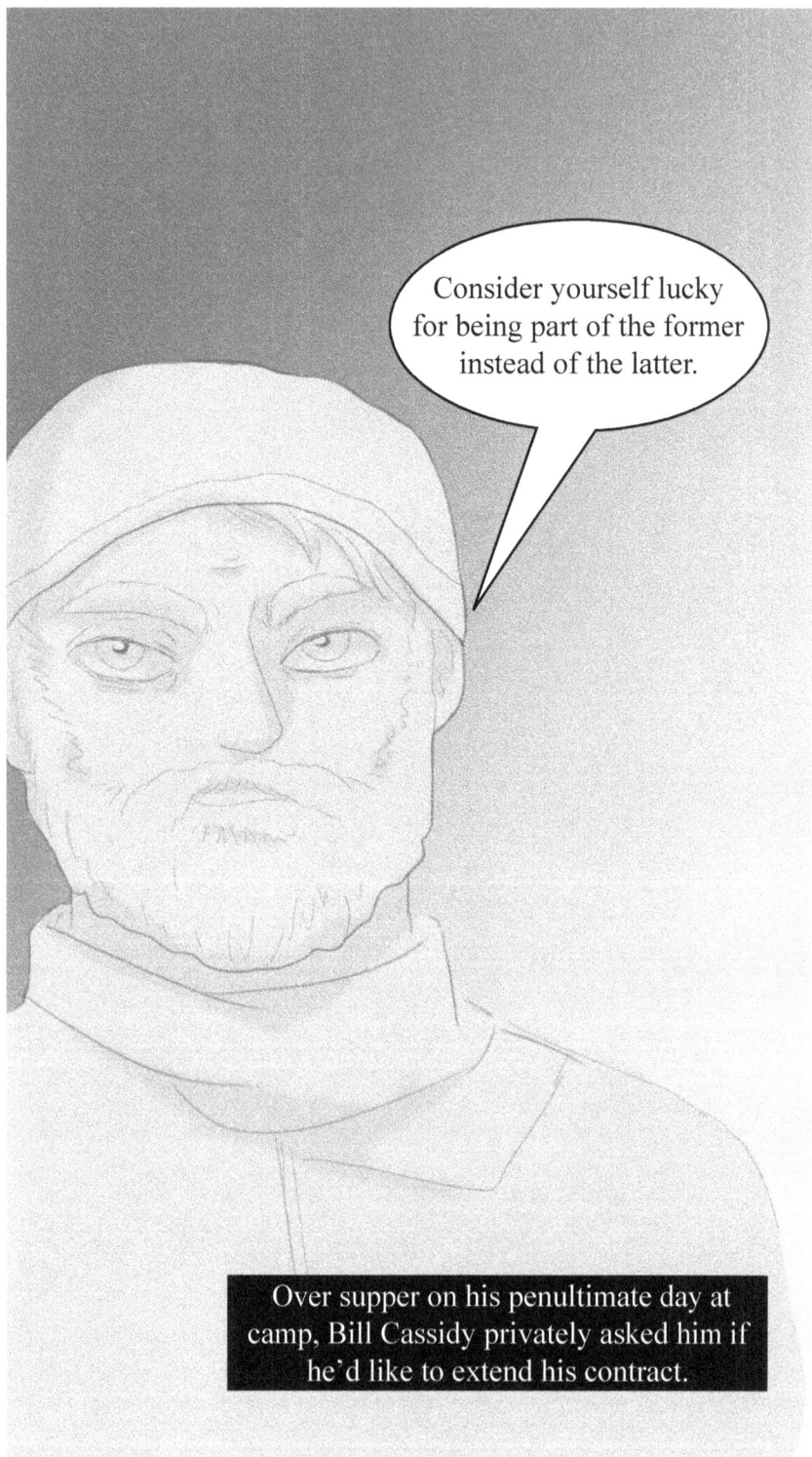

Austin wanted more, but he was tired of trying. His brain and body hurt, and so did the realization that these people didn't care about his well-being.

I can't. I have to go back to school.

I think you should reconsider. I'd hate to have to train someone else.

Austin wanted to be more upset that Bill couldn't comprehend his pain.

Thank you for the offer. But I can't take another break. They'll want me back.

He felt defeated.

The crew said their goodbyes, wishing him well in school.

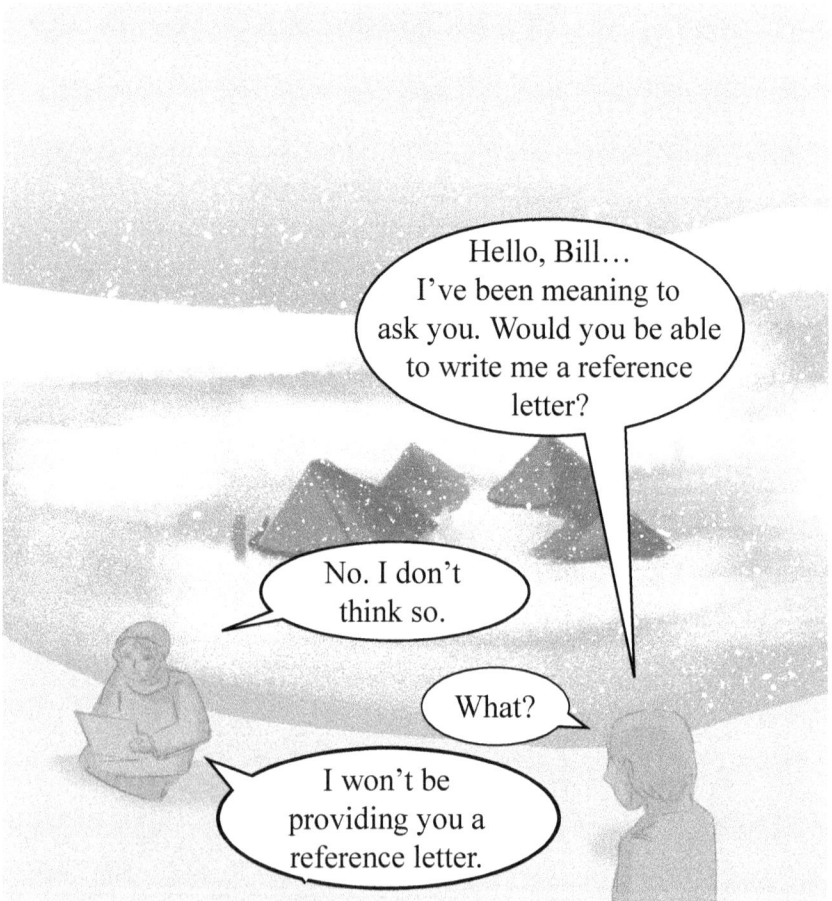

Hello, Bill... I've been meaning to ask you. Would you be able to write me a reference letter?

No. I don't think so.

What?

I won't be providing you a reference letter.

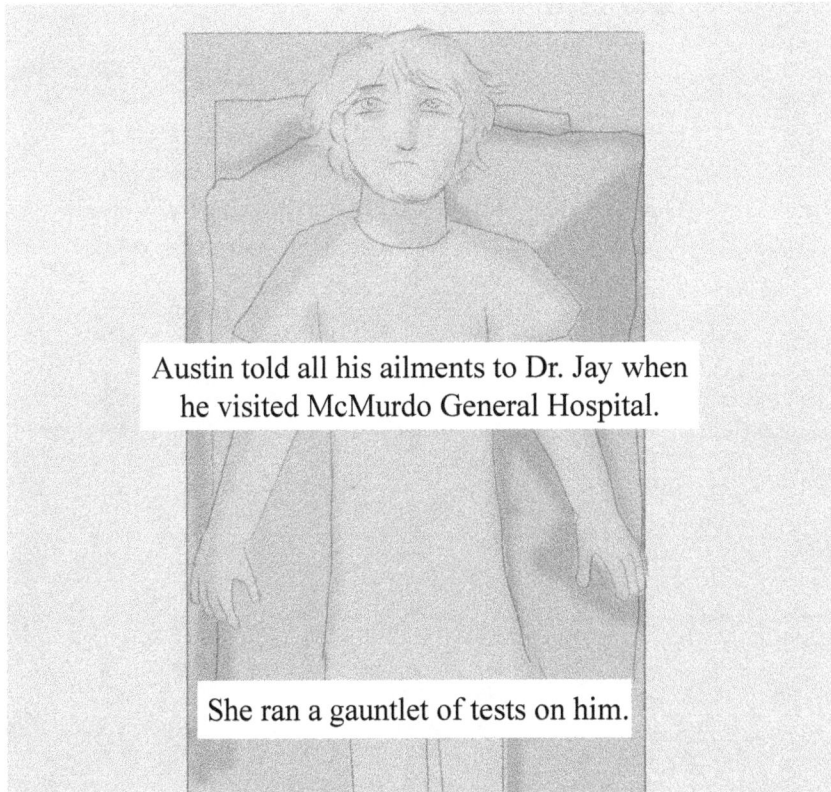

Austin told all his ailments to Dr. Jay when he visited McMurdo General Hospital.

She ran a gauntlet of tests on him.

I'm afraid you have extensive damage to your legs.

You said it was normal to have damage.

It is... to a certain degree. The cold has destroyed a lot of the surface-level tissue. There's a large amount of deep-tissue scarring. Long-term exposure to the cold causes damage, but the damage was aggravated by your weight loss.

The damage is much deeper than the surface. There's a high likelihood that your legs will need to be amputated by the time you reach age forty.

My *legs?*

Amputate my legs?

Amputate. *My* legs?

The day before he was set to leave, a letter from his uncle Francis arrived,

cheerily welcoming him to stay in New Zealand.

Austin read the letter again and again, especially the last line:

Can't wait to hear about your trip to Antarctica!
—Uncle Francis

At the end of February, Austin
caught the C-130 Hercules aircraft
back to Christchurch.

He turned to look out his window
and caught a slight reflection
of his face and almost didn't
recognize himself.

All at once, Austin realized
how tired he actually was.

He tried reading his book: but
his brain was in a fog.

The Salinas Valley is in Northern
California. It is a long narrow swale
between two ranges of mountains, and
the Salinas River winds and twists up
the center until it falls at last into
Monterey Bay.

I remember my childhood names for
grasses and secret flowers. I
remember where a toad may live and
what time the birds awaken in the
summer—and what trees and seasons
smelled like—how people looked and
walked and smelled even. The
memory of odors is very rich.

His uncle was picking him up from the airport.

He closed his eyes, and saw the grainy blown up meteorite-less images of the Antarctic sites.

Austin? I almost didn't recognize you!

I guess I probably look a little different.

Austin, are you okay?

I don't really feel like myself right now. After some proper rest, I'll be right as rain.

I'm excited to hear all about your adventures!

It wasn't an adventure. It was dangerous work.

CHAPTER 15

Family Matters

When Austin woke, it was night time, but everything was loud. Birds of all kinds were making noises.

He'd gotten used to the silence of the Antarctic.

Hello?

Hello, my name is Austin Mardon. I'm a PhD candidate in the Educational Geography department. I've just finished my research term with the ANSMET program. I'm wondering when I'm supposed to return to my studies.

Yes, Austin. Please hold a moment.

There's gotta be something you can do. Call back later.

My friends are having a dinner party tonight. I said you would come.

You don't have to, but maybe it's good timing. Take your mind off everything.

The last thing in the world Austin felt like doing was going to a dinner party, but his uncle had been so nice to him. He decided to call his dad.

Austin, you don't sound right. You sound sick or something.

I just haven't been sleeping well. I'm fine.

I'll make some calls to your school okay? Just enjoy being in New Zealand right now.

Austin felt a homesickness he hadn't felt while he was in Antarctica. He missed his childhood bed.

Time to get up for the dinner party. You've been sleeping since you got here. It's getting ridiculous.

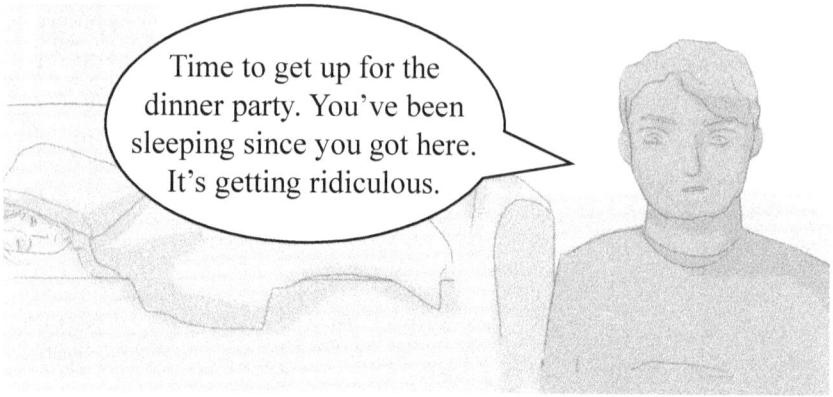

By the time he was showered and dressed, he was completely exhausted.

You didn't even shave?

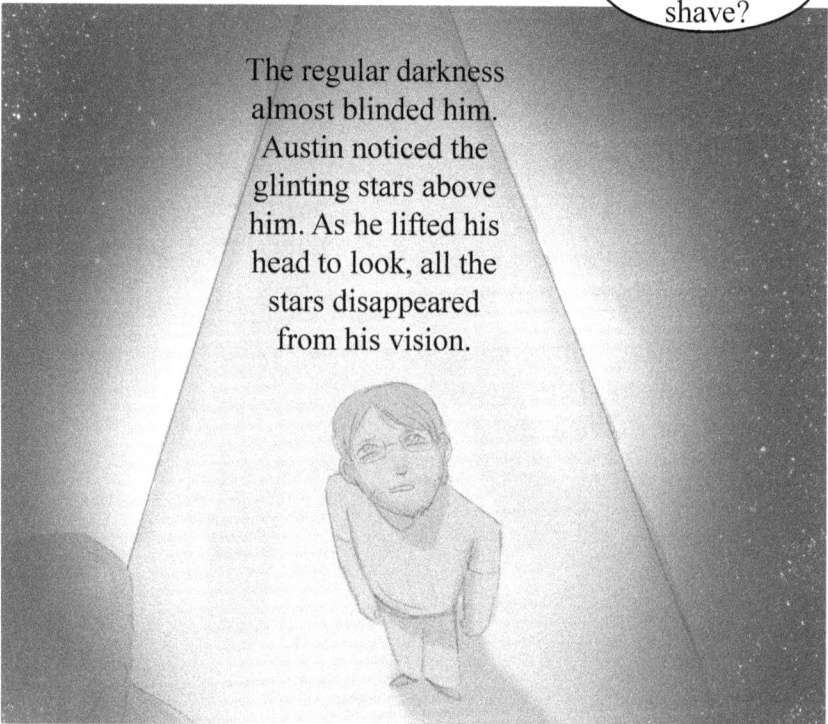

The regular darkness almost blinded him. Austin noticed the glinting stars above him. As he lifted his head to look, all the stars disappeared from his vision.

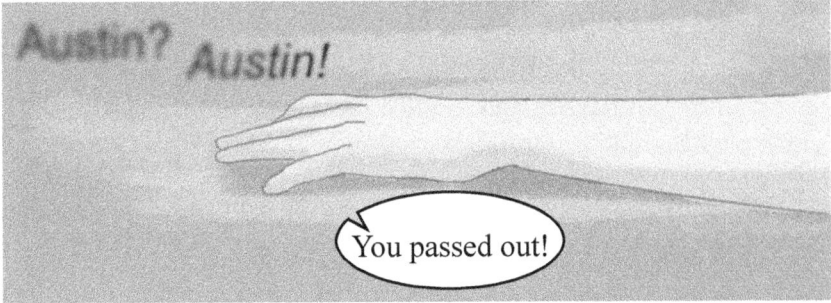

I slept in the snow and ice for months! In the sun and in the cold. That doesn't even make sense. It was always sunny, and always cold.
I almost died. I almost fell to my death, picking rocks, and it was all for nothing.
I'm going back to nothing. My research failed. I failed my classes. I am a failure, and so are you for knowing me.

You're just like your father. *You're just like him.* Obsessed with success and failure. And I'm sorry you almost died, but guess what? You lived. You're alive. Not like Cassidy's mum, hey? I remember that from your letter. You're not going back to nothing. You're going back to your *parents.*

Austin sat on the ground and held his head. He wished he'd fallen into that fucking crevasse.

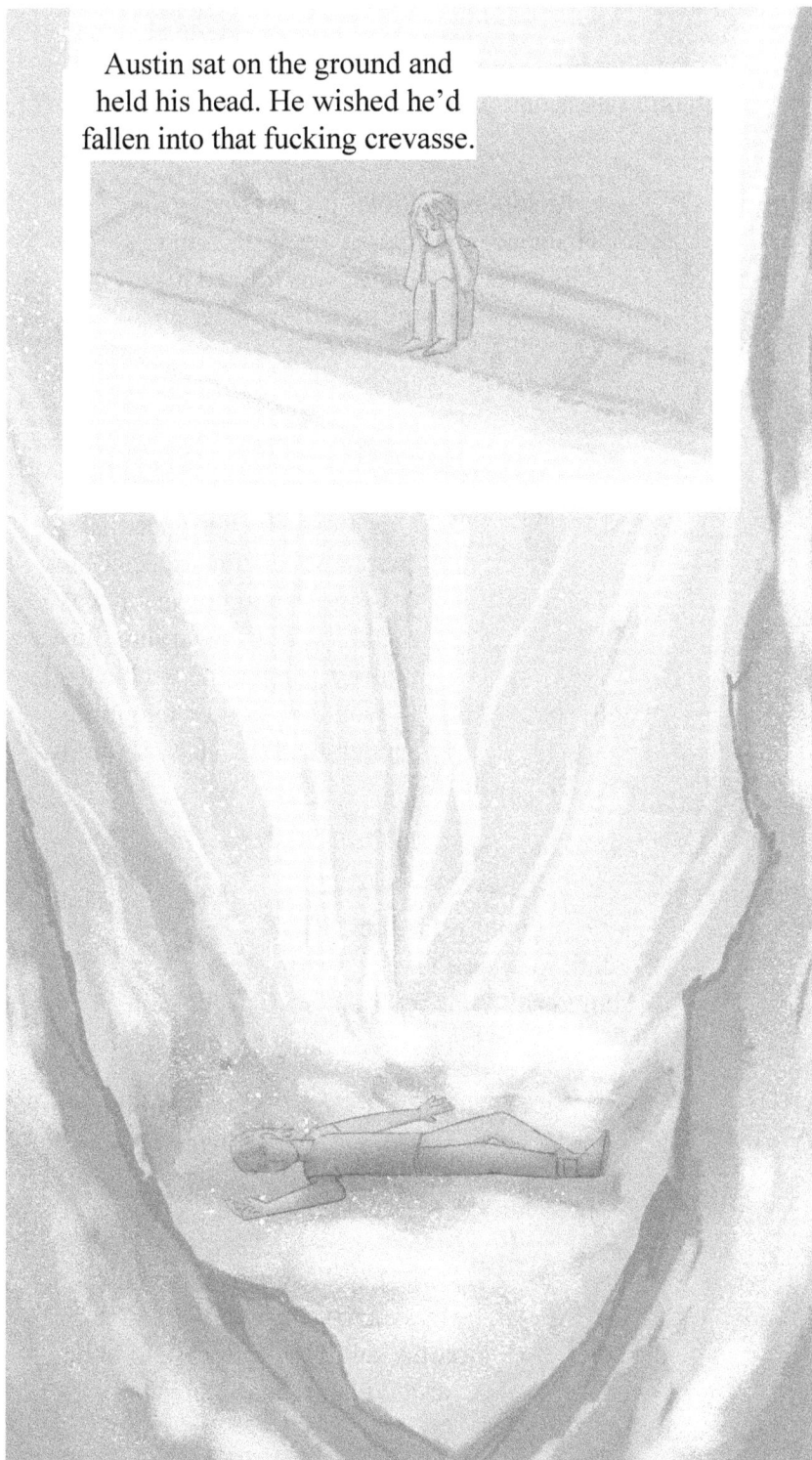

The next couple of days were tough on Francis and Austin.

Austin's health wasn't improving. His headaches weren't getting better. His sense of balance was off and his legs were still incredibly sore.

Francis grew to see Austin as more of a nuisance than a nephew. Austin suspected that Francis thought Austin was faking or exaggerating his injuries. He had hoped his uncle would be kinder, and more understanding. He was family.

I think it'd be best if you left. You aren't well, Austin. You should call your parents. Get a flight back home.

Don't pretend to care now.

I do care. Austin. You haven't been exactly… agreeable. I don't want my family coming home to be around aggressive behavior.

So Austin took his
things and left.

After ten minutes of walking, he found
it: the statue of Robert Falcon Scott in
the center of the park square.

Bill Cassidy once told him that
he visited the statue every time
he went to New Zealand, and it
only occurred to Austin now to
think that was strange.

Robert Falcon Scott didn't seem like the kind of guy that Cassidy would consider to be a good role-model, with all the controversy and "adventure" attitude surrounding him.

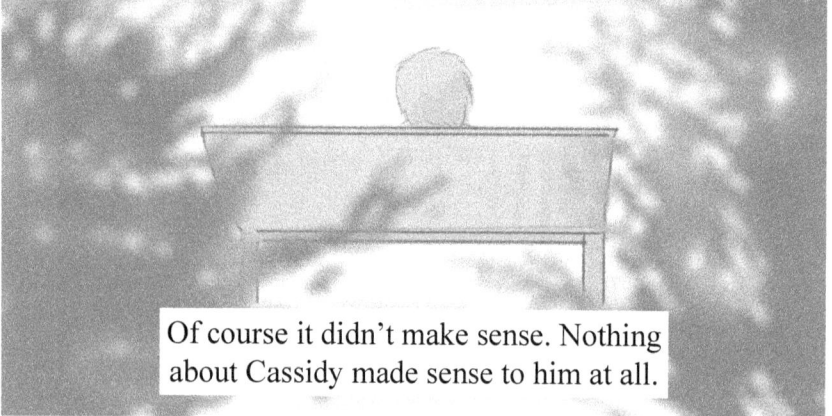

Of course it didn't make sense. Nothing about Cassidy made sense to him at all.

Austin found a phone booth at the side of another petrol station. He dropped in his coins and listened to the ringing until his uncle in Santa Barbara answered. When Austin eventually hung up the phone, he felt much better. He then booked a flight to the United States.

Though his flight wasn't leaving until midnight, Austin made his way to his terminal gate where he waited. Something he was used to doing by then.

CHAPTER 16

Santa Barbara

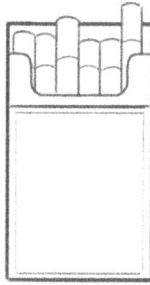

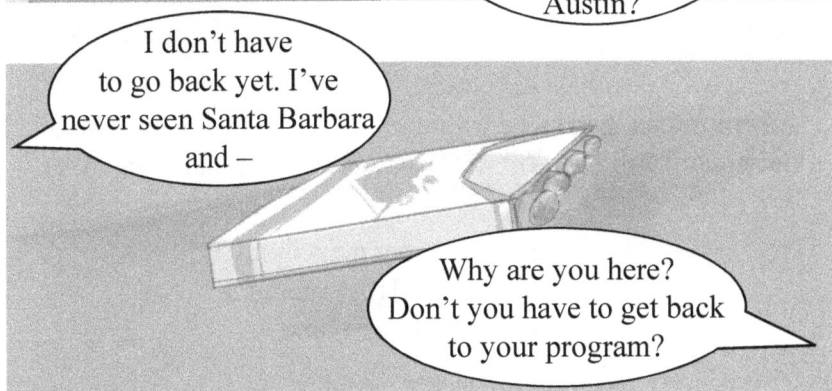

No. I was kicked out.

And what's wrong with your legs?

I don't know. The doctor in McMurdo said they're damaged from the cold.

Austin, go home. You're not well.

Austin fumed, headache forgotten for the moment because of his anger at Bill Cassidy, at Texas A&M, at Francis. And Troy.

But the thing that made him angriest was that Troy was right. He needed to go home.

CHAPTER 17

Home Again

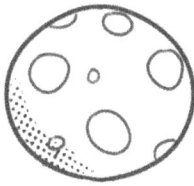

When he arrived in Calgary, Austin decided he would walk to the bus station, saving money for a ticket to Lethbridge.

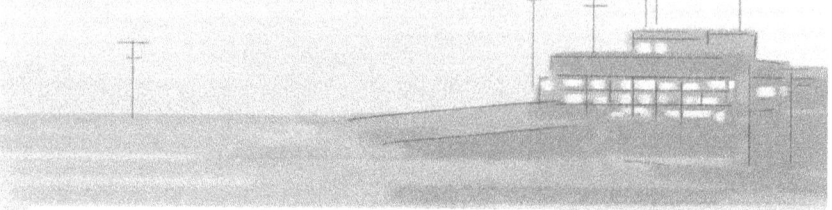

He was walking down the highway for an hour before he realized that he actually had no idea where the bus station was.

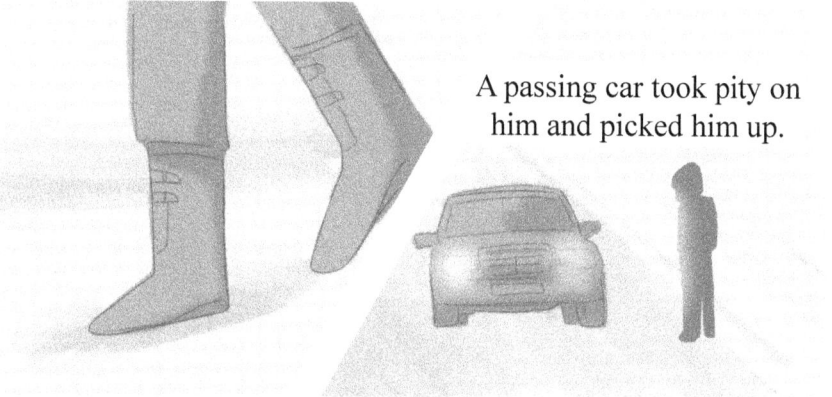

A passing car took pity on him and picked him up.

The radio played a song his dad had sung during his childhood.

I want to ride to the ridge where the West commences,
And gaze at the moon 'til I lose my senses.
I can't look at hobbles, and I can't stand fences,
Don't fence me in...

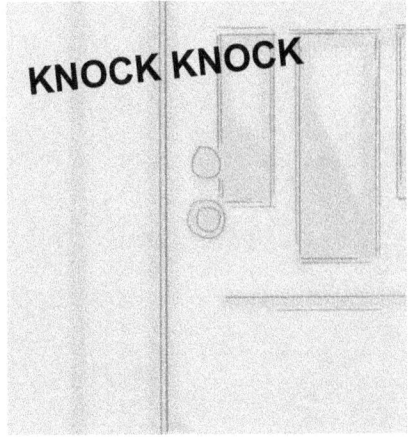

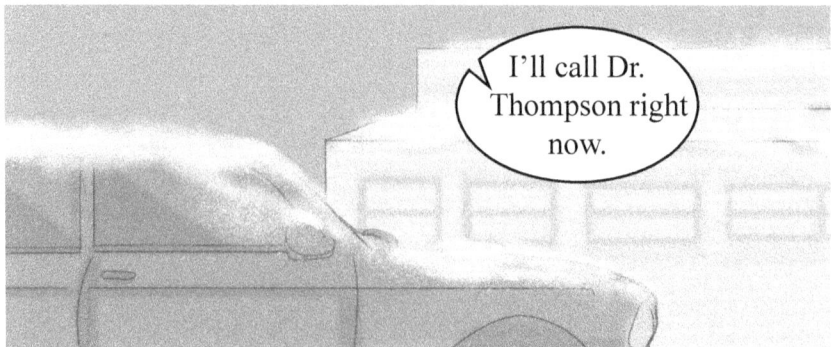

Austin went to his family doctor the next day for an urgent appointment.

He was hooked up to an IV, while the nurses did some blood work, urine and stool samples.

After the samples had been sent to the lab, he waited with his dad.

Dr. Thompson told them the news: Austin
had mild nerve damage in his legs, but he
wouldn't need anything amputated.

He needed to rest, but he'd eventually just
get better. He also suffered altitude sickness,
but that would level out after some time.

What great
news! You just
need a little bit of
time.

After several weeks, he regained full use of his legs, though he walked with a bit of a limp, and his headaches had gone completely.

Though he could count again, his mind still felt foggy sometimes.

Ernest never said anything about whether he'd gotten anywhere calling Austin's school. Austin knew he'd gotten nowhere.

He got a job as a dishwasher at a local restaurant. They let him do his work without bothering him.

He was more and more disinterested in the activities of everyday life.

He found solace in the monotony of going to work and back home again.

Austin still thought about his expulsion from Texas A&M.
The thought no longer angered him as much.

EAST OF EDEN

He started thinking about
appealing their decision, the
thought of needing to fight
invaded his mind more and
more frequently.

He tried to will himself
back to the way he was
before he left.

He put some weight back on, and
finished reading East of Eden,
but he knew he had changed.

Some nights in the pitch
blackness of his bedroom,
Austin could be found sleeping
with a t-shirt over his face.

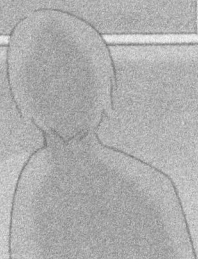

Other nights he made hot
chocolate, and stayed up
late to stare at the moon.

Austin is a Member of the Order of Canada, and has met the Pope. He has schizophrenia; he is also an advocate for mental-health awareness in Edmonton and throughout Alberta.

The creation of the Antarctic Institute of Canada, its subsidiary, and this particular book were all inspired by Austin's only foray into the Antarctic. The research that instigated Austin's participation in the expedition--aerial photography in the service of extracting meteorites from Antarctica--saw failing results. Austin believes that the failures and harsh environmental stresses in McMurdo, and later at home and university, brought about his late-onset schizophrenia.

Austin and Catherine met through a Catholic dating site. She was an American, a retired lawyer and ex-drill team member, who had been assaulted by members of the KKK for testifying against them in court. After a dispensation from the church, thousands of exchanged emails, and the perusal/ approval of the Canadian government of the legitimacy of their relationship, Catherine moved to Canada and married Austin. They have been together ever since, and live with their adopted sons in Edmonton.

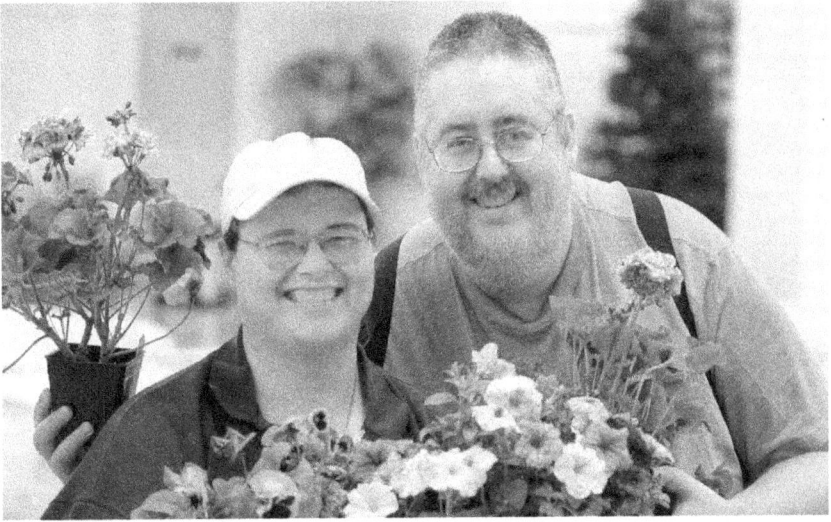

Austin admires Elon Musk's work, and believes that climate change will eventually force humanity to colonize other planets. Colonizing other planets, Austin says, has a certain amount of romanticism to it. It's an adventure narrative, like Christopher Columbus. A man of 55 years, Austin is still full of dreams and aspirations.

Though he doesn't believe that he will ever have the chance, Austin acutely desires one day to set foot on the moon.

The Taste of Frozen Tears has been adapted into a graphic novel and illustrated by Clare Dalton, who lives in Edmonton. When Austin asked if she wanted to make an illustrated version of the story, she said yes immediately. The fact that she'd never made a comic longer than two pages mattered very little in that moment. Clare loves art and storytelling, so naturally she loved this project and the wonderful opportunity to bring Austin's tale to life in an new genre. She plans to continue pursuing her passion for illustration and hopes to one day create a graphic novel with her own story and characters.

www.ingramcontent.com/pod-product-compliance
Lightning Source LLC
Chambersburg PA
CBHW032003080426
42735CB00007B/500